WINDOWS OF

peace

peace

WINDOWS OF WORSHIP™

When I'm
LONGING FOR GOD

:: DEVOTIONAL JOURNAL ::

Greg Allen ▪ Rick Rusaw ▪ Dan Stuecher
Paul S. Williams, *Editor*

Standard
PUBLISHING

© 2004 CNI Holdings Corp., Windows of Worship is a Trademark of
Christian Network, Inc.

Published by Standard Publishing, Cincinnati, Ohio. A division of Standex
International Corporation. Printed in China.

Cover and interior design by Rule29.

Discover where to watch *Worship* in your town by logging on to
www.Worship.net.

ISBN 0-7847-1521-1

09 08 07 06 05 04   9 8 7 6 5 4 3 2 1

We were made to worship...

The first song I remember Grandma Stone singing to me was "Jesus Loves Me." As a three-year-old I sat on her lap on the front porch swing and asked her to sing it over and over again. Before my daughter Jana could speak, she hummed the same tune, its melody unmistakable as she played on the family room floor. We were made to worship.

To worship God is to walk through the shadows into a familiar welcoming place, where the fire never dies and the light is soft and glowing. To worship God is to know we are truly home, acting on a desire deep in our souls. Long before we rationally understand the truth of Christ, we want to praise someone or something for bringing love and beauty, joy and hope into the world.

At the Christian Network, our desire is simple. Whether through the written page or the television screen, we hope these words and images will draw you to worship, as we thank our creator for breathing life and love into his creation.

PAUL S. WILLIAMS
Chairman of the Board of Stewards
The Christian Network, Inc.

Celebrate Mystery and Wonder

Praise the LORD, O my soul.

O LORD my God, you are very great;

> *you are clothed with splendor and majesty.*

He wraps himself in light as with a garment;

> *he stretches out the heavens like a tent*

> *and lays the beams of his upper chambers on their waters.*

He makes the clouds his chariot

> *and rides on the wings of the wind.*

He makes winds his messengers,

> *flames of fire his servants.*

He set the earth on its foundations;

> *it can never be moved.*

You covered it with the deep as with a garment;

> *the waters stood above the mountains.*

PSALM 104:1-6

CELEBRATE MYSTERY AND WONDER

I must admit I was never very good at science. On more than one occasion, when I couldn't remember that Au was the symbol for gold or where the last Ice Age stopped its advance, a science grade kept me from getting straight As on my report card. So I'm certainly not going to object when philosophers suggest we are leaving the Age of Science or the Modern Age. It doesn't bother me a bit.

It's not that scientific discoveries aren't still being made every day or that science and technology aren't moving into new frontiers. They are. It's that we have begun to see what science can and cannot do. As the writer Wendell Berry suggests, "We are learning to know precisely the location of our genes, but significant numbers of us don't know the whereabouts of our children."

The Age of Science has made us more informed humans, but it has not made us better parents, spouses, or friends. "I've got to check my e-mail before we sit down for dinner. It'll only take a couple minutes." By the time you're done, the casserole is cold and headed back to the microwave. In the Age of Science, there's no time to watch the stars or contemplate the mystery and wonder of the universe. In fact, in the Age of Science mysteries aren't tolerated at all. They are problems to be solved in the objective environment of the laboratory. "Wonder" itself has been marked for extinction because there is always a scientific explanation for mystery and wonder. Anything that can't be logically explained is to be stuffed into a forgotten closet in a seldom-used guest room.

But a world with no mystery and wonder is a place I'd rather not be. It's a world in which I'm invited to see myself as a complicated machine or chemical reaction but nothing more. But is that all I am—just some randomly firing neurons?

It was Thomas Edison who said, "We don't even begin to understand one percent about 99 percent of anything." Edison was a bright man who seemed to know the limitations of science. Pascal also said it well: "The heart has its reasons that reason does not know." There are mysteries that will never be solved. If we have eyes to see, there is glorious wonder abounding. The one who hung the stars and makes light dance across the northern sky holds the patent on mystery and wonder, and he doesn't want us to lose sight of them.

I was on a dock by the bay with hundreds of other vacationers, watching the sun set across the waters of the west. As the orange globe slipped beneath the surf, there was at first a faint, then unmistakably growing, wave of applause that grew to a grand crescendo and continued for a very long time. Mystery and wonder were celebrated, ushering all into God's courts of praise.

—*Paul S. Williams*

Have you been caught up in the Age of Science—trying to explain everything through reason? Why or why not?

How can you celebrate the mystery and wonder of God's world today? Write down your reflections as you contemplate God's creation.

_____

_____

_____

_____

_____

9

_____

_____

_____

_____

_____

_____

_____

_____

Boring Prayers

The Spirit helps us in our weakness. We do not know what we

ought to pray for, but the Spirit himself intercedes for us with

groans that words cannot express. And he who searches our

hearts knows the mind of the Spirit, because the Spirit intercedes

for the saints in accordance with God's will.

ROMANS 8:26, 27

BORING PRAYERS

Now please don't take up your hammer and bludgeon me to death, but I have to say it. I find a significant number of prayers, both public and private, to be incredibly boring. I do understand this is a subject people are not encouraged to bring to light for some very compelling reasons. Critiquing people's public or private communication with God is a pretty dicey proposition. It just about guarantees a couple of angry letters. So let me admit from the beginning that I'm including my own prayers in my critique. Sometimes my own communication with God, public and private, seems trite, even boring. So, please indulge me as I think on paper.

It seems to me some people put about the same thought into the language of their prayers as they put into the answers they give a telemarketer. They take advantage of the idea that God is their friend, their good buddy. I guess the problem I have is that I discern a big difference between God and me. A gap so great that *friend* doesn't seem to be the most appropriate term to define the relationship. *Worship* is what should define our relationship with God. And with worship comes awe. And with awe comes very carefully crafted language—no endless litany of personal requests for physical assistance, no constant repetitions— but thoughtful poetry and prose from my heart to God's.

I would love to have heard T. S. Eliot pray, or C.S. Lewis.
Barbara Brown Taylor's homilies sound like one giant prayer,
and I don't doubt Kathleen Norris is worth listening to in a
Wednesday evening prayer meeting. They know what to do with
words. But just because my vocabulary is limited doesn't mean
I can't work a little harder at showing my heavenly Father some
respect when I address him.

I am often disappointed by my own prayers. I figure God has to
be bored. I know I am. But that's when I remember God's Spirit.
I may be the writer, but the Spirit is the translator. The Spirit
takes my 12 "Dear Heavenly Fathers," all spoken within the
confines of a single paragraph, and turns them into a supplica-
tion of awe and beauty as he whispers into the Father's ear.
I don't have to worry about the language of my prayers. The Spirit
has taken care of that for me.

Yes, it would be nice if I always approached God with reverence
and chose carefully both the words and subjects of my prayers.
But things being as they are, I imagine God's happy to be hearing
from me at all.

—Paul S. Williams

Do you find your prayers boring and repetitious? When you speak to God, do you feel awe or a dull sense of duty?

Does your perspective change when you realize that the Holy Spirit is acting as your translator—converting your human words into heavenly words and conveying them straight to the throne of God?

_____

_____

_____

_____

_____

15

_____

_____

_____

_____

_____

_____

_____

_____

One Great Love

Because your love is better than life,

my lips will glorify you.

I will praise you as long as I live,

and in your name I will lift up my hands.

PSALM 63:3, 4

ONE GREAT LOVE

Time and time again we are reminded, although we rarely allow the reminder to register, that relationships are the real catalysts for growth in our lives. We are easily distracted to think that achievement or material wealth might be the source of our purpose, but that simply is not true.

The portly, bearded, eccentric classical composer Johannes Brahms, most often photographed during his older years, was once a 20-year-old, socially awkward, but extremely talented young musician looking to make his way in the world. Through the influence of a friend, Brahms was introduced to the musical giant Robert Schumann and his wife, Clara. It would not be the powerful compositions, the eventual success, or even the prestige of his worldwide popularity, but the relationship Brahms would slowly develop with Clara, a lovely woman nearly 15 years his senior, that would change the course of his life.

Invited to play in the Schumann home, Brahms made a striking impression on everyone present, but it was Schumann's wife, Clara, who would be captivated by the childlike, backward young musician and his powerful rendition of his own compositions. The Schumanns lent their heartiest endorsement of Brahms to all the musical circles throughout Germany. In a single stroke the anonymity of the young Brahms was gone forever.

But Robert Schumann was struggling with unseen demons. About a year after meeting Brahms, a combination of physical liabilities and emotional imbalance drove Schumann to attempt suicide. He was institutionalized, leaving Clara on the verge of despair. She was expecting their seventh child and had no financial support. Several friends rushed to her side, Brahms among them. For almost three years Brahms ran errands for Clara, taught her piano students when she was ill, spent time with her children, and helped in any way he could.

All the while, in the secret chambers of his heart, the relationship with Clara evolved from friendship to love, though no
evidence remotely suggests that there was ever any impropriety.
But his affections raged within him to the point that he left for
weeks at a time trying to sort them out and deal with his
conflicted emotions.

Even after Robert Schumann died, Brahms did not openly pursue a romantic or marital relationship with Clara. For the next
40 years their lives went in somewhat separate directions but
they remained the closest of lifelong friends. By his own admis-
sion, Brahms measured every other relationship in his life by
the depth of his love for her. No amount of success or popularity
would ever take priority over this one abiding relationship.

Suppose for a moment you and I would choose to love God the
way Johannes Brahms loved Clara Schumann. Our lives would
change dramatically from that moment forward. We would
experience a focused energy, a driving purpose, possibly an
uncharacteristic discipline that only a love of such depth can
produce. Every thought, decision, and relationship would be
measured against our love commitment to him. We would
find *meaning.*

Jesus declared that the greatest of all commandments is to "Love
the Lord your God with all your heart and with all your soul and
with all your mind" (Matthew 22:37). Why? Because he knew
that in that single relationship the true meaning of life is found.

—Dan Stuecher

What is the one great love in your life? What are you committed to above all else?

If God is not your one great love, why not? How might your life change if you made him your focus above everything else?

_____

_____

_____

_____

_____

_____

_____

_____

_____

_____

_____

_____

Out of the Fog

You, O LORD, keep my lamp burning;

my God turns my darkness into light.

PSALM 18:28

OUT OF THE FOG

When I first entered ministry, and was way too young to know anything, I always liked to read psalms in the services of our little congregation. But I would only read the upbeat psalms. I had no idea what to do with verses like Psalm 89:46, "How long, O LORD? Will you hide yourself forever? How long will your wrath burn like fire?" So I did what I did with a lot of things I didn't understand in life up to that time—I ignored the dark psalms. I ignored the angry, depressed, vengeful psalms.

But now I'm much older, a little wiser, and I know what to do with those so-called dark psalms.

Some of us are steady and even. Some of us are moody. The moody among us know the feeling of despair—a feeling captured in Psalm 38. Guilt, anger, and shame in wave after wave are expressed—"My heart pounds, my strength fails me; even the light has gone from my eyes" (v. 10). Psalm 38 is an entire 22 verses of pain, inviting me to allow the depth of my own pain to be expressed. It is a lament of darkness. It is real life.

And that's exactly why I need to read it. That psalm illustrates some of the days of my life. People who call the religion of Abraham, Isaac, Jacob, and Jesus a pie-in-the-sky religion haven't read much of the Bible. If anything, the psalms are earthy and often dark. I have prayed that final verse of Psalm 38 more than once—"Come quickly to help me, O Lord my Savior." Many of the dark psalms could be summarized into a mournful phrase: "Life is hard, and then you die."

But that's not where the psalms end. Yes, they do invite us to acknowledge that life is hard, but even at their darkest the psalms offer a postscript. And what is that hopeful P.S.? It is: "And yet!"

"Life is hard, and then you die. And yet!"

In verse 15 of Psalm 38, in the midst of the darkness, we find the "and yet." It's a tiny sliver of light. "I wait for you, O LORD; you will answer, O Lord my God."

I was visiting a famous lighthouse in Maine once, but when we arrived the fog was so thick there was nothing to be seen. The rock and lighthouse were there, not 100 yards across the water on a rock outcropping, but my eyes could see nothing but dark clouds and the periodic pulsing of the searchlight. But strangely, that light was enough. It was real. It told me there was beauty very close, though I couldn't see it or touch it. All I had was the awful darkness. But through the fog, the light pierced and gave me hope.

25

And so it is with Psalm 38, and the other verses that speak of the dark night of the soul. They acknowledge that it is a foggy world out there. But they shine with the light of the lighthouse. They speak of the darkness I know, and they show that occasional glimmer of hope, and that's more than enough to take me through the dark and foggy night into a bright new morning, where things will surely be seen more clearly.

—Paul S. Williams

What is the "fog" in your life—those things that make it hard for
you to see through to joy and hope?

_____

_____

_____

_____

_____

_____

_____

_____

_____

_____

_____

_____

_____

_____

Write a prayer, asking God for his light in the midst of your darkness. Even though you may not be able to see him through the fog, he is there. Look for his light and you will find it.

_____

_____

_____

_____

_____

_____

_____

_____

_____

_____

_____

_____

_____

_____

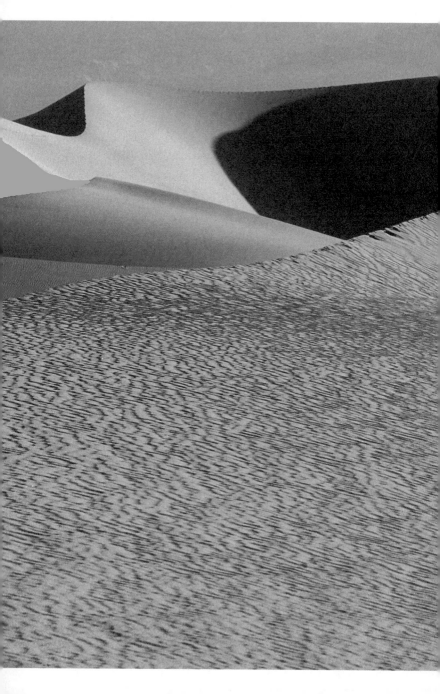

peace

Singers in Front

Sing the glory of his name;

make his praise glorious!

Say to God, "How awesome are your deeds!

So great is your power

that your enemies cringe before you.

All the earth bows down to you;

they sing praise to you,

they sing praise to your name."

PSALM 66:2-4

SINGERS IN FRONT

I absolutely love music. I have my favorites, but if it's done with
excellence, I generally like all sorts of styles, from an adagio for
strings to a hard-driving guitar and drumbeat. Music stirs my
emotions, and I like that. I think God does too. Jesus told us to
love God with our hearts as well as with our minds. The heart is
the seedbed of our emotions, and nothing stirs the heart like
music. Throughout the Bible, when people needed to be
reminded where their strength was, they were encouraged to
sing praises to God and worship him with all their hearts.

The Old Testament psalms are filled with encouragement to use
music to draw us closer to God so we might serve him more
faithfully, worship him more fully, and win big battles. "What?"
you say. Yes. God used music to help armies win battles.

In the Old Testament, singers were often placed in front of the
army when God's people headed into the enemy camp. The
singers sang praises to God as the army prepared to fight. The
enemy saw a ragtag, inferior army headed straight toward them,
with a collection of folks leading the way singing, "Our God Is
an Awesome God" (or the Hebrew equivalent of the day). They
must have thought it was a ridiculous sight. But before the day
was over, those enemy armies didn't think the singers were
ridiculous at all.

So why *singers?* Did God dislike their music so much he decided to put the worship team first, so they'd be the first to die in battle, and he wouldn't have to listen to their infernal music any longer? Hardly. No, God wanted the enemies to know it was the almighty God who reigned. And he wanted his own armies to place their trust in him, not in themselves. And of course, time after time, when God's army followed his plan of worshiping him first, not only did the singers live, but God's army triumphed as well.

God's method of going into battle might be a good reminder for me. I face enemies every day—skeptics, naysayers, my own unhealthy desires. To win battles against such foes I must not trust in my own ability, but in God's strength. And I know no better way to do that than by singing praises to him, because no matter how great my enemies, with God's praise on my lips and his worship in my heart, the battle is already won.

—Greg Allen

What battles are you facing right now? How are you fighting them?

Use your concordance or a Bible search program to find verses
on praise and worship and write down a few that speak to you.
Apply them to your battles by writing them in your own words.

_____

_____

_____

_____

_____

_____

_____

_____

_____

_____

_____

_____

_____

Cast Your Nets on the Other Side

Simon Peter, Thomas (called Didymus), Nathanael from Cana in Galilee, the sons of Zebedee, and two other disciples were together. "I'm going out to fish," Simon Peter told them, and they said, "We'll go with you." So they went out and got into the boat, but that night they caught nothing. Early in the morning, Jesus stood on the shore, but the disciples did not realize that it was Jesus. . . . He said, "Throw your net on the right side of the boat and you will find some." When they did, they were unable to haul the net in because of the large number of fish.

Then the disciple whom Jesus loved said to Peter, "It is the Lord!"

JOHN 21:2-4, 6, 7

CAST YOUR NETS ON THE OTHER SIDE

I've taken a few vacations where the stated goal was fishing. But in reality, all I really wanted to do was nothing, while holding a fishing pole. The pull on the end of the fishing line was just the unexpected excitement of the day. When your friends say they've "gone fishing" you can be pretty sure that's the kind of trip they're talking about.

Jesus had a group of friends who were fishermen. But they weren't sport fishermen intent on a lazy day down at the old fishin' hole. They were commercial fisherman. Commercial fishing is, in fact, the most dangerous profession on Earth. Even today, more fishermen die in the line of duty than in any other occupation. The life of a commercial fisherman is not easy.

Jesus took these fishermen away from the sea. For three years they learned from him and watched in amazement as he taught them to be fishers of *men.* But then Jesus was killed, and they returned to the only thing they knew—boats and nets and rough water.

The men were out fishing one night, but after a full night of hard work, their nets came up empty time and time again. After three years of a wild ride with Jesus, they were back to the life of the sea, and they weren't catching anything. They were frustrated and tired.

To make matters worse, back on the shore someone was suggesting they cast their nets on the other side of the boat. That's just what they needed—fishing advice from a landlubber. But, frankly, what did they have to lose? They cast their nets on the other side and came up with 153 fish. They decided to take another look at the man on the shore, and John exclaimed, "It is the Lord!" Peter jumped in the water and left the others to haul the catch back to shore. Jesus was preparing breakfast for his friends.

The last time the disciples had eaten with Jesus was at the Last Supper, right before his death. But now they were seaside with the risen Lord, as he prepared the first meal of their new life together. Barbara Brown Taylor calls it a resurrection breakfast prepared by the only one who knew the recipe.

In the entire Gospel of John, the author records his own words only twice. The first time is when Jesus said one of the disciples would betray him. John said, "Is it I?" He knew, as I know about myself, that he was fully capable of betraying the Lord on any given day. And the second time he recorded his own words? It was this occasion. When they realized the man on the shore was none other than the risen Lord, it was John who stated the obvious—"It is the Lord!"

The moral of the story: Keep your eyes and ears and heart open to the truth. Who knows when you, in a time of defeat and uncertainty, might hear a stranger call to you from across the open water and say, "Cast your nets on the other side"? And what once was a day of fruitless struggle becomes a day of laughter and tears of joy.

—Paul S. Williams

Are you facing a time of frustration and confusion when noth-ing is going right and God seems far away? Write about your struggle here.

_____

_____

_____

_____

_____

_____

_____

_____

_____

_____

_____

_____

_____

Write a prayer, giving your frustration to the Lord. Ask him to speak to you and to help you see a better way through the long night. He promises to be there for you!

_____

_____

_____

_____

_____

_____

_____

_____

_____

_____

_____

_____

_____

_____

With Ears to Hear

I will listen to what God the LORD will say;

he promises peace to his people, his saints.

PSALM 85:8

WITH EARS TO HEAR

I am a host for a television program called *Worship Network*, and I am also a worship leader at my own home church. I very much appreciate the joy of good worship. But what is it that makes worship great?

I'd say great worship happens when I am totally consumed by the God I worship. When I view God's mercy in my life—knowing that he has chosen to forgive my pride, my self-centeredness, and all my sins—then I become consumed by God's grace and I am drawn to worship him.

Jesus once told a woman he met that the key to good worship was to drink from the right well. We can try quenching our thirst at any number of wrong wells, but we'll always be thirsty again. But Jesus said that there was a well where you could drink and never be thirsty again.

I was worshiping at a concert hall in the mountains of Colorado. I was in the seventh row, and they were in the sixth. A mom and her two children were just in front of me and slightly to my left. I could see everything that happened. The music was exceptional and inspiring, but the two children didn't know that. They were both deaf. As soon as I realized the little brother and sister couldn't hear, I began to wonder what you would wonder—what would it be like to see people sing and musicians play, yet sit in total silence?

The children watched the big screen as the words were displayed. Better still, their mom communicated the words to them through a sign language that was beautiful and poetic. The little girl gave her mom her undivided attention. When a song spoke of praying a blessing over people, the mom laid her hand on her son's head, as if she were doing just that, praying a blessing. As the children's eyes filled with the joy of worship, my eyes filled with tears of wonder.

I love good worship, but I have to work at it—I have to work to stay focused on living in the presence of God's Holy Spirit. I don't know if I've ever worshiped more fully than when I watched that mother and her two young children. All three were worshiping God in a beautiful way.

And yet there *I* stood, fully able to hear every glorious sound coming from the musicians, the song leader, and the audience—voices lifted triumphantly to God in one accord. I heard every note.

Those children didn't have the ability to hear; yet through their mother they heard. I do have ears to hear. So let me never neglect worshiping you, O Lord. Let me hear you loud and clear, Lord, let me hear you loud and clear.

—Greg Allen

What is your worship like? Are you ever completely consumed by God? If so, describe what that is like. If not, what might help you worship God more fully?

Worship God on paper here. List as many reasons to praise God as you can.

_____

_____

_____

_____

_____

_____

_____

_____

_____

_____

_____

_____

Rules for Living

Whoever would love life

   and see good days

must keep his tongue from evil

   and his lips from deceitful speech.

He must turn from evil and do good;

   he must seek peace and pursue it.

For the eyes of the Lord are on the righteous

   and his ears are attentive to their prayer.

1 Peter 3:10-12

RULES FOR LIVING

Years ago I was speaking at a conference in downtown Chicago. As we were preparing to leave the convention hall, the chief of hotel security warned us that there recently had been a number of muggings near the hotel. He then gave us tips on how to navigate safely around the city.

"First, don't act lost, even if you are. If you do get lost, duck into a store or restaurant until you get your bearings. Second, move with speed and confidence, even if you are lost. Don't act like a tourist staring up at the buildings or searching a map. Third, don't make direct eye contact. Be polite, but don't engage a stranger. And finally, remove your name tag when you leave the hotel." I suppose those were great rules for navigating safely in a strange city—but I'm not sure they're great rules for living my life.

Rule #1: Don't act lost. But what if I *am* lost? Isn't it funny how we like to act as if we know where we're going, even when we don't?

Rule #2: Move with speed and confidence. But the truth is, if I don't know where I'm going, all the speed and confidence in the world are useless.

Rule #3: Don't make direct eye contact. Avoid any connection with other human beings? Try to do it all alone? This is definitely *not* how we were made to live.

Rule #4: Remove your name tag. Hey, anonymity feels safe. If I don't get too close to people, maybe they won't see how deep my needs really are—being vulnerable is just too scary.

The rules for staying safe on a big city street may work in Chicago, but they are lousy rules for living my life.

It's true that life is filled with challenges, no matter who you are. There are thrills and spills, opportunities and setbacks. We all live in a world with laughter and tears, joy and sorrow. The world is a real place, where I need to live in a real community with other real people. Living fully isn't about fake confidence or plastic smiles or flimsy superman capes. I get lost now and again, and it's time I quit hiding that truth.

There is much about God that remains a mystery to me, but of one thing I am certain: God loves and cares for me completely, no matter what. And the sooner we all quit playing games and learn to rest in his love, and the love of each other, the happier we'll all be.

—*Rick Rusaw*

What rules do you live by? Think about how you live your life every day and write down a few of the rules you follow.

Are the rules you live by the rules God has called you to follow?
If not, what habits should you change so that you are leading
your life according to God's plan?

_____

_____

_____

_____

_____

_____

_____

_____

_____

_____

_____

_____

_____

_____

_____

'Tis Midnight

Then Jesus went with his disciples to a place called Gethsemane, and he said to them, "Sit here while I go over there and pray."

He took Peter and the two sons of Zebedee along with him, and he began to be sorrowful and troubled.

Then he said to them, "My soul is overwhelmed with sorrow to the point of death. Stay here and keep watch with me." Going a little farther, he fell with his face to the ground and prayed, "My Father, if it is possible, may this cup be taken from me. Yet not as I will, but as you will."

MATTHEW 26:36-39

'TIS MIDNIGHT

Sunday evening church services were a regular feature of my childhood. There were congregational singing, an offering, a 20-minute sermon, and Communion for all those who had been unable to attend morning services. About every third week, the Sunday evening Communion hymn was the same, "'Tis Midnight, and on Olive's Brow."

We sang one verse to begin the Communion service:

> *'Tis midnight, and on Olive's brow,*
> *The star is dimmed that lately shown;*
> *'Tis midnight in the garden now,*
> *The suffering Savior prays alone.*

Those words stirred feelings inside me long before I knew the depth of their meaning or the story to which they refer. Jesus was in the garden praying. He was sweating drops of blood. He was ministered to by angels. He was preparing to be betrayed.

You can't be betrayed by your enemies. You expect an enemy to do you in. You can't be betrayed by a stranger. You have no idea how a stranger is likely to behave. No, you can be betrayed only by a family member or friend. To have someone you thought would stand with you turn his or her back on you—that is betrayal.

I wish I knew nothing of betrayal. But I am human and, painfully, I know what it is to be betrayed. You pass through all the stages of any emotional wound. First, you deny. "I can't believe he did it!" you cry, hoping for a different explanation that will let your friend or family member off the hook.

Then comes the anger, lots of anger. And after the anger, comes the depression. And finally, by the grace of God you come to acceptance. But how do we get from denial to acceptance? How do we get past our own hurt to understand what has caused our friend to betray us in the first place? The truth is that betrayal often has little to do with us. We're just in the wrong place at the wrong time. Often what causes betrayal is solely in the heart of the betrayer. How do we, the wounded, get inside that heart of the one who wounded us, to see the pain that took our friend to that awful place? I think Jesus showed us in the garden how to do that.

The betrayal was coming. Jesus' natural response was to turn to the only one who would never let him down. Luke tells us he went, *as usual,* to the Mount of Olives. Jesus made it a practice to talk regularly with the one person who would never betray him—his Father. So in the richness of that bond, Jesus took this greatest of sorrows to his Father in prayer. Through the agony, the Father sent angels to care for his Son, and the Son remembered that the Father's love was enough to take him through even this darkest night of the soul.

And God will take *us* through our dark nights as well. We are not alone.

—*Paul S. Williams*

Think about what Jesus suffered for you, not only on the cross, but also in the garden that dark night before his death. Reflect on what it means to you that Jesus suffered physically, mentally, and spiritually for you.

God has promised to be with you in your struggles just as he was with his Son in the midst of his agony. Go into your "garden" and write a prayer, pouring out your needs and hurts to God. He will come and minister to you.

Immortal Beloved

*God, the blessed and only Ruler, the King of kings and Lord of
lords . . . alone is immortal and . . . lives in unapproachable light,
whom no one has seen or can see. To him be honor and might
forever. Amen.*

1 TIMOTHY 6:15, 16

IMMORTAL BELOVED

She could have been any one of several women. For over 200 years historians, biographers, and music scholars have presented what they believed to be conclusive evidence as to her identity, and still nobody knows for sure who she was. A motion picture has been marketed by her title and, though produced with excellence, the movie's attempt to identify her is preposterous. Just who is it we're trying to discover? She is the one Ludwig van Beethoven called his "Immortal Beloved."

Beethoven never married. We can only speculate that may have had something to do with difficulties in his family of origin or the eccentricities of his personality. It certainly was not because he disliked the company of women. He experienced deep affection for several women during his adult life—most of them, however, unavailable or uninterested. But there was one woman who clearly captivated his heart.

When he was 42 years old he wrote to her with words that could only have come from thoughts and passions springing from complete emotional surrender. He called her his Immortal Beloved. The letter begins, "My Angel, my all, my very self." In the body of the letter are such lines as:

> *"Love demands all, and rightly so."*
> *"To face life I must live altogether with you or never see you."*
> *"Oh, why must one be separated from her who is so dear?"*

He closes with:

> *"However much you love me—my love for you is even greater . . ."*

This letter was found in a secret drawer of a bureau that belonged to Beethoven. It was undated and not addressed. Had it ever been sent? Had the love of his life never even seen the letter? Sometime after the letter would have been written, a friend noticed Beethoven wearing a gold ring on his finger. Somewhat jokingly the friend asked if he had any loves other than his Immortal Beloved. He did not answer. Nor would he ever. He carried the secret of her identity to his grave.

Beethoven, the composer of such passionate music, was true to form in his love life as well. And to this day we still do not know who his Immortal Beloved really was. Was she his beloved? Most certainly. Reading the letter will leave little doubt about that. But was she immortal? Hardly.

There is only one Immortal Beloved, and his identity is no secret. He is the King of kings and the Lord of lords. He is the beloved of God. He has extended a sacrificial love to us that transcends our understanding. And he is immortal for he conquered death. He has always been and will always be. And he has sent us a passionate love letter that we would do well to read— the Bible. Then we can discover for ourselves that he is truly *our* Immortal Beloved.

—*Dan Stuecher*

Who is your beloved? What makes that person the focus of your deep love?

We are the beloved of God—write him a love letter here,
expressing your love in return.

Meaningless

"Meaningless! Meaningless!" says the Teacher.

"Everything is meaningless!" . . .

Now all has been heard;

here is the conclusion of the matter:

Fear God and keep his commandments,

for this is the whole duty of man.

ECCLESIASTES 12:8, 13

MEANINGLESS

I was proud, I was tired, and I was finished. I had a wonderful sense of accomplishment as I surveyed my finely manicured lawn. I was hot, but the iced tea, (favorite brand, sweet, no lemon) was cooling me. I was tired but resting comfortably in my hammock. Then it hit me—in five days I'd have to do it all over again! My evenly mowed lawn would be ragged, the weeds would be visible and my hammock would be empty because once again I would be pushing and sweating to landscape a lawn that would need it again in *another* five days. Futility! It's all meaningless!

These days I'm learning that some things are here today, gone tomorrow—things that were never intended to give ultimate meaning to our lives—like yard work, my job, my hobbies. And I plan to sip more tea and take more time to think about the things that really do give my life significance. There is room in the hammock for you too.

Solomon had spent a lot of time in a hammock thinking through these things. He considered his accomplishments, pleasures, wealth, and knowledge. He built entire cities, amassed the equivalent of 200 billion dollars a year, and was smarter, wiser, and more knowledgeable than any philosopher anywhere. He enjoyed the finest food and drink and more private pleasure than is appropriate to speak of in a devotional journal. But Solomon said his life was empty, futile, and void of real meaning.

He used the phrase *under the sun* several times in the book of Ecclesiastes. As he rocked in his hammock, he noted that everything under the sun was limited, finite, and incapable of giving a person real significance. Everything, he said, is here today, gone tomorrow. So he kept swinging in that hammock and considering what really does give us a reason for living.

Another man who pondered life was Job. He had all a man needed: a great wife and family, real estate, and wealth. But he lost it all—family, lands, and money—in one fateful day. As he considered his lot, he had the chance to contemplate what brings true significance, meaning, and purpose in life. And through it all Job learned a profound truth. He said, "The LORD gave and the LORD has taken away; may the name of the LORD be praised" (Job 1:21). Job learned the true meaning of life. We were made to give glory to the Lord, no matter what.

As I consider the yard work, my career, my retirement plan, and my most precious family, I pray for the perspective that reminds me that things under the sun are here today, gone tomorrow, but the one who is above the sun is eternal and worthy of my praise.

—Greg Allen

What parts of your life sometimes feel meaningless? Is that because they really are?

What gives your life meaning? Are those things truly meaningful in the light of eternity?

_____

_____

_____

_____

_____

_____

_____

_____

_____

_____

_____

_____

The Word Incarnate

In the beginning was the Word, and the Word was with God, and the Word was God. He was with God in the beginning. Through him all things were made; without him nothing was made that has been made. In him was life, and that life was the light of men. The light shines in the darkness, but the darkness has not understood it. . . . The true light that gives light to every man was coming into the world. He was in the world, and though the world was made through him, the world did not recognize him. He came to that which was his own, but his own did not receive him. Yet to all who received him, to those who believed in his name, he gave the right to become children of God—children born not of natural descent, nor of human decision or a husband's will, but born of God.

JOHN 1:1-5, 9-13

THE WORD INCARNATE

I make my living with words. I string about 350 of them together each week for a magazine column I write. It takes about 700 words threaded together in a meaningful fashion (I hope) to write the devotions for books like this. I write, write, and rewrite as I try to find a voice for what I'm feeling on this journey of life. All told, I write about 50,000 words or more a year. Words have been good to me.

Sometimes I write words for a book or for the magazine I help edit. Sometimes I speak words instead of writing them. I memorize about 3,000 words and call the finished product a sermon. I like memorizing my sermons. I write out a message, and then as I go about the process of memorizing the words I've put on paper, I tend to forget stuff. The stuff I forget is usually extraneous to the message. That's why I forgot it in the first place. I begin with about 30 minutes' worth of words. By the time I've completed the memorizing, I have about 22 minutes' worth left. No one ever complains about a shortened sermon.

I'm amazed by how marvelously some people use words. There are only 267 of them in the Gettysburg Address; yet when I read just the first six words, "Four score and seven years ago," a chill goes up my spine. "To be or not to be." Those six words take you straight into the turmoil of Shakespeare's *Hamlet*. And with three simple words, "It is finished," Jesus ushered in a whole new world.

Whether writing for the magazine I edit, for a book, or for a sermon, sometimes words just aren't enough. The first time I reached the top of Colorado's 14,255-foot tall Long's Peak, I could find no words to describe the beauty, so I took pictures instead—five of them. According to the old saying, that was 5,000 words' worth.

I felt the same way when I first set eyes on all three of my children and the first time I sang praise songs in a crowd of 10,000. Sometimes words aren't enough.

I suppose God knew that all along. So he made the Word flesh— the Word that was in the beginning, the Word that was with God, and the Word that was God. And the Word dwelt among us. And that incarnate Word is the truth that changes the world.

—*Paul S. Williams*

The Word of God caused the whole universe to come into being. What does it mean to you to realize the power in that Word came to Earth in the bodily form of Jesus?

What can you do to convey the truth of the Word incarnate, Jesus Christ, to those around you who don't know his love?

_____

_____

_____

_____

_____

_____

_____

_____

_____

_____

_____

Choices

"What shall I do, then, with Jesus who is called Christ?"
Pilate asked.
They all answered, "Crucify him!"
"Why? What crime has he committed?" asked Pilate.
But they shouted all the louder, "Crucify him!"
When Pilate saw that he was getting nowhere, but that instead
an uproar was starting, he took water and washed his hands in
front of the crowd. "I am innocent of this man's blood," he said.
"It is your responsibility!"
All the people answered, "Let his blood be on us and on our
children!"
Then he released Barabbas to them. But he had Jesus flogged, and
handed him over to be crucified.

MATTHEW 27:22-26

CHOICES

Our lives are often defined by our choices. There are plenty of big choices, but the reality is that our journey is usually characterized by the piling up of little choices that ultimately determine the course for our lives. There is an old Chinese proverb that says, "If we keep heading in the same direction, we are likely to end up where we are headed." Of course, the important question is, do we want to go where we are headed? Often in the middle of our lives, we find ourselves saying, "How did I end up here, and is this really the direction I want to go?"

The Roman governor Pilate was in a position of influence. He had the opportunity to choose and set the direction for many. History reveals the results of a choice he made that he didn't want to make in the first place. The big choice he made, the choice that Scripture records for us, was informed by the little choices he had made along the way. I have a friend in politics who says that it is difficult to go very far politically without trying to please everyone. Whether that is true or not, Pilate certainly wasn't the last politico to make his choice based on opinion polls, where popularity is chosen over truth. Pilate's choice to sentence Jesus to death appeared not to be easy for him, but in the end it was *his* choice.

The longest journey I have ever made was short in distance—
less than two feet. It was the journey from my head to my heart.
We can know the truth but it is quite another matter to live it.
It is one thing for us to believe; it is another to let that belief
change us. We can have God's grace but is still often quite
difficult to live gracefully.

Our choice to follow God, to accept his gift, is a choice from the
head *and* the heart. The Greeks and the Hebrews saw the heart
as the seat of intellect, emotion, and will. It was the place where
the choices of life were made. Life is the piling up of our choices—
some big, some small, but all setting a direction. Where are your
choices taking you?

For the last few years I have been praying this very simple prayer
each morning, "Lord, today, all day long, I will have plenty of
opportunities to choose. Help me to choose well. Help me to
choose you."

—Rick Rusaw

What choices did you make today? How might these choices affect your life in the future?

What choice have you made about Jesus? Are you, like Pilate, choosing to see him as the world sees him—a troublemaker? Or are you seeing him as he truly is—your Savior?

_____

_____

_____

_____

_____

_____

_____

_____

_____

_____

_____

_____

_____

I Wonder As I Wander

For to us a child is born,

to us a son is given,

and the government will be on his shoulders.

And he will be called

Wonderful Counselor, Mighty God,

Everlasting Father, Prince of Peace.

ISAIAH 9:6

I WONDER AS I WANDER

I see a flock of robins on the Southern State Parkway around the fourth week of January every single year. What makes that unusual is that I live on Long Island, New York. This particular flock seems a little confused about the start of spring.

I notice the same seasonal confusion happens every fall among Americans. The Christmas selling season begins earlier and earlier every year. It has been moved back from Thanksgiving to Halloween. Not long ago I saw a Christmas sales poster the first week of October. Before long the Christmas selling season will move back to Labor Day—one last swim before we head off to the mall for our first Christmas sale!

One pundit recently suggested it that it won't be long before the average Christmas spending in America will be over $1,000 per person. The average is several hundred dollars per person now. That figures up to lots of gifts people can't afford, given to people who may well return them anyway. Fifty percent of all buying in America takes place at Christmastime. For some industries, Christmas purchases make up 90 percent of their sales. No wonder the Christmas season keeps starting earlier and earlier.

But try as hard as we might, it seems we still haven't completely ruined the season. That is a miracle in itself. Through all the glitz and glamour shines a mystery that overshadows the brightest of Christmas ornaments—the truth that God came to live among us.

John Jacob Niles tells of the time a small group of traveling evangelists came and set up their tents on the courthouse square of his town. They hung their laundry on the Confederate monument and began to preach on the courthouse square, until the county commissioner made them pack up and leave. But before they left, John heard the daughter of one itinerant evangelist sing a song he had never heard before:

> *I wonder as I wander out under the sky,*
> *Why Jesus our Savior did come for to die,*
> *For poor, lonely people like you and like I,*
> *I wonder as I wander out under the sky.*

Niles asked her where she had heard that song. She didn't remember. "Is there more to it?" he asked.

"Not as far as I know," was her reply.

So John Jacob Niles took the song, elaborated on it, and published it. This song slows us down in the middle of the craziness of the season and reminds us of the beauty and mystery that will never die, no matter how hard the marketers try to kill it. Through all the crass commercialization shines the mystery of Christ.

—*Paul S. Williams*

What is Christmas like for your family? Have you fallen into the commercialization of the holiday?

This Christmas, how can you bring the true light of Christ into the center of your celebrations? Reflect on this and write down some specific, practical things you will plan to incorporate into the holiday this year.

_____

_____

_____

_____

_____

_____

_____

_____

_____

_____

_____

_____

The Birds of the Air

Praise the LORD from the earth,

   you great sea creatures and all ocean depths,

lightning and hail, snow and clouds,

   stormy winds that do his bidding,

you mountains and all hills,

   fruit trees and all cedars,

wild animals and all cattle,

   small creatures and flying birds,

kings of the earth and all nations,

   you princes and all rulers on earth,

young men and maidens,

   old men and children.

PSALM 148:7-12

THE BIRDS OF THE AIR

Some people hear God with a shout. Pascal, on one occasion, was so overpowered by the presence of God that he wrote down the date and time and sewed them into the coat he wore for the rest of his life. Now *that's* an epiphany.

But I haven't experienced God that way. I've always heard God in a whisper or seen him in the golden ember of a campfire or felt him in a timely embrace.

When I run in the early hours of the morning during the winter months, the air is cool and crisp, and the silence is deafening. As spring approaches, the birds return, and their sweet sounds break the morning stillness. On dark spring mornings the killdeers give out their protective call as they seek to draw intruders away from their ground nests. As daylight comes earlier it is not unusual to hear a red-tailed hawk call to her young. I hear the songs of robins, bluebirds, and chickadees, and I wonder what their songs might say if I could understand them.

In *The Magician's Nephew*, C. S. Lewis tells of the creation of the mythical state of Narnia, a place where the animals and trees talk. In this particular book Lewis writes about a song the creator sings that cannot be compared to anything we've heard in this present world. I wonder, do the birds sing a similar song we humans cannot understand? Do they sing because they know something we don't?

Sitting in the backyard during the summer I see the humming-birds as they flit from flower to feeder and back again. Their wings beat so rapidly it sometimes looks like they are fixed in the air. The shimmering reds and greens of the males stand in stark contrast to the white trim on my neighbor's porch. Once in a while one will stop for a moment in the top of the young maple tree, and I catch a fleeting glimpse of red before it flies off again, noiselessly.

As the fall and winter come, my morning runs grow quiet as the birds follow their instincts south. The Canada geese follow their democratic dance, with first one bird leading the flying *V*, and then another moving in to take his place.

I wonder . . . do hawks and sparrows, hummingbirds and Canada geese know that they sing at the pleasure of their creator, or am I the only one who hears voices of praise?

—Myron Williams for Paul S. Williams

Do you think that birds and other creatures somehow know their creator?

_____

_____

_____

_____

_____

_____

_____

_____

_____

_____

_____

_____

_____

Look through your Bible for verses on creation and the glory of God. What do these verses seem to say about creation in relation to its creator?

_____

_____

_____

_____

_____

_____

93

_____

_____

_____

_____

_____

_____

_____

A Kingdom of Relationships

So when [Jesus and his disciples] met together, they asked him,
"Lord, are you at this time going to restore the kingdom to Israel?"
He said to them: "It is not for you to know the times or dates the
Father has set by his own authority. But you will receive power
when the Holy Spirit comes on you; and you will be my witnesses
in Jerusalem, and in all Judea and Samaria, and to the ends of
the earth."

After he said this, he was taken up before their very eyes, and a
cloud hid him from their sight. They were looking intently up into
the sky as he was going, when suddenly two men dressed in white
stood beside them.

"Men of Galilee," they said, "why do you stand here looking into the
sky? This same Jesus, who has been taken from you into heaven,
will come back in the same way you have seen him go into heaven."

ACTS 1:6-11

A KINGDOM OF RELATIONSHIPS

They say the three jobs of a corporate CEO are vision, financing, and succession. Where is the company going? How are we going to pay for it? And who will take my place when I'm gone?

I wonder if Jesus ever asked those questions? After his resurrection, when he was ready to return to Heaven, from all appearances it looked like his work was done. His followers understood the vision. They were willing to pay for it, with their own lives if necessary. And those same followers, aided by his own Spirit, would take his place when he was gone. Everything was set for the future of Christ's church. Or was it?

Jesus' followers had seen him, alive and resurrected, after his crucifixion. They saw with their own eyes. Now they were ready for Jesus to become king, to take over the world and run it as it ought to be run. No one would get in his way. Not in Jerusalem. Not in Israel. Not anywhere. He would rule the universe, and his followers would be his political appointees.

But there was someone who stood in the way of those desires, someone who had no interest in political rule. That someone was Jesus himself.

Jesus didn't come to be an earthly king, but it was always difficult for his followers to understand that. They wanted him to defeat his enemies and bring about a new government. And they wanted to have powerful positions within that government. But Jesus had a different idea.

After Jesus' resurrection, his followers gathered with him outside the city of Jerusalem. Jesus told them he was leaving. But they interrupted to ask him one more question. "Is it time now?" they said. "Is it time now for you to create a political kingdom?" They wanted it so badly they could taste it.

I can just see Jesus turning up to the heavens and announcing to the angels waiting to take him home—"Sorry, folks, this'll take just one more minute." And then he turned to his followers and said one last time that his kingdom was not about politics or power. His kingdom was about something else. It was about relationships.

Jesus didn't come to take over the world as political ruler. He came to teach the people of the world how to love one another. He came to establish a kingdom, all right—a kingdom of relationships, built on loving God and loving each other. And when the followers of Jesus finally understood that, then they were ready to start the church that would bear the name of Christ. And Jesus was ready to head back home, his work on Earth finally done.

—Paul S. Williams

97

Is your church working to further God's kingdom by loving others and loving God, or is it trying to use politics and causes instead?

_____

_____

_____

_____

_____

_____

_____

_____

_____

_____

_____

_____

_____

How can you live your life as a relationship builder? Write down some practical and specific ideas.

_____

_____

_____

_____

_____

_____

_____

_____

_____

_____

_____

_____

_____

Through the Suffering

Have mercy on me, O God, have mercy on me,

> *for in you my soul takes refuge.*

I will take refuge in the shadow of your wings

> *until the disaster has passed.*

I cry out to God Most High,

> *to God, who fulfills his purpose for me.*

He sends from heaven and saves me,

> *rebuking those who hotly pursue me;*
> *God sends his love and his faithfulness.*

PSALM 57:1-3

THROUGH THE SUFFERING

In A.D. 80, during the reign of Titus, the Roman Colosseum was completed. It could seat nearly 50,000 people. It stood four stories tall, 620 feet long, and 513 feet wide. Awnings could be hung from the walls to protect spectators from the sun.

The Colosseum was a place of entertainment. But when regular entertainment, including games and feasts, didn't prove enough to satisfy the crowds, things got ugly. Gladiators fought there. Christians were killed there. Cages were installed beneath the arena floor for men and animals. Slaves turned cranks that lifted the cages from the grimy depths to the arena floor.

The Roman Colosseum is now a ruin of stone and mortar, a tourist attraction. Thousands converge to view the ruins and imagine the carnage and death that took place there. Separated from the actual events by a couple thousand years, our 21st century experience seems far removed from the suffering that took place inside those walls. But I know better. Suffering is always with us. Evil always makes its presence known. But evil, thank God, is not the final word.

Years before the Colosseum was built during the high point of the Roman Empire, David, the king of Israel, spoke of suffering—the kind of suffering known only too well to those who died on the arena floor of the Colosseum. In Psalm 57, David calls out to God for mercy and deliverance in the face of frightening perils. David knew what he was talking about too—at the time he was hiding in a cave because King Saul was out to kill him.

Throughout the psalms we see suffering is a part of the human condition. It doesn't matter how good or righteous, kind or generous, law-abiding or loving we are. We all will suffer. Maybe our suffering won't be as great as that of those who died in the Roman Colosseum, but we all will suffer, nevertheless.

Notice in Psalm 57 that David does not promise that God will take away our suffering. What is promised is that God will be present with us through our suffering. The key word is *through*. He will not abandon us. He will never leave us. He cannot stop loving us. And that is enough for David. It allows him to end the psalm with these beautiful words:

> *For great is your love, reaching to the heavens;*
> *your faithfulness reaches to the skies.*
> *Be exalted, O God, above the heavens;*
> *let your glory be over all the earth.*

—*Paul S. Williams*

Read all of Psalm 57 from your favorite Bible translation. Make two lists: the dangers and trials David suffered, and his attitude toward God in the midst of the suffering.

Write your own psalm—pouring out your fears and suffering. Finish by praising God for his care and presence with you through it all.

_____

_____

_____

_____

_____

_____

_____

_____

_____

_____

_____

_____

_____

Whom Should I Thank?

O LORD, our Lord,

> *how majestic is your name in all the earth!*

You have set your glory

> *above the heavens. . . .*

When I consider your heavens,

> *the work of your fingers,*

the moon and the stars,

> *which you have set in place,*

what is man that you are mindful of him,

> *the son of man that you care for him?*

PSALM 8:1, 3, 4

WHOM SHOULD I THANK?

From the time I was old enough to understand evil, I began to question the existence of God. How could a loving God arbitrarily allow one guy to be murdered by thieves while another won the lottery? How could the little kid down the block from me be in an iron lung with polio, while I ran carefree through the neighborhood?

I went to a Christian college not so much out of conviction as out of a hope that somebody could make some sense of all this mess. I got a few answers, but for the most part, I just ended up with more questions. It seemed only the good died young, while mean-spirited people went on forever. Was there even a God at all?

I couldn't find a satisfactory explanation for all the pain, suffering, and evil that existed in the world, so I decided there was no God. And for quite a long time I remained a skeptic. I wanted very much to believe that this world merely had evolved from nothing, from some primordial soup. But hard as I tried, I was unable to sustain such a cynical approach to life.

First, I had children. They were so beautiful and full of something that didn't come from my wife and me. How could I explain that? That such beauty just evolved seemed a shallow and completely inadequate answer.

And then there were all the wonders of nature my eyes had taken in. The first time I saw the ocean, I was mesmerized by the cresting waves crashing into weathered cliffs. It was winter when I first set my eyes on the Rockies, and the snow-covered peaks were breathtaking. There is awe in the beauty of nature that reaches deep down inside and grabs the soul. It pulls you upward, ever upward, into something that can only be called worship. Your soul demands *someone* to thank, because in spite of all the evil and suffering, there is also unfathomable beauty and outrageous love.

I've traveled to 43 American states, six Canadian provinces, and several other countries. I've seen Arizona deserts bloom with life in the cool spring. I've trekked to the top of 14,000-foot Colorado peaks. I've seen the hills of Newfoundland covered with May snow, and I've seen 2,000-year-old olive trees on the Italian countryside. I've gone running through the woods of Vienna and kayaked the waters of the Atlantic. And after a lifetime of such striking variety and breathtaking beauty, I've turned in my official badge of skepticism to embrace the wonder of it all.

I quit fighting what my heart had known all along—that there is someone to thank for all the good and beauty. And you know what? I've been thanking God ever since.

—Paul S. Williams

What experiences in your life have caused your soul to well up with thanks? Describe some of the sights, sounds, tastes, smells, and feelings that have revealed God's majesty to you.

Write down your praises to God for all the beauty he has put into your life.

_____

_____

_____

_____

_____

_____

_____

_____

_____

_____

_____

_____

_____

The Thing You Fear

For you did not receive a spirit that makes you a slave again to fear, but you received the Spirit of sonship. And by him we cry, "Abba, Father."

ROMANS 8:15

THE THING YOU FEAR

Written 1,500 years ago, the Old English poem *Beowulf* tells a story as relevant today as it was then. The king of Denmark was desperate for someone who could destroy Grendel, a swamp monster who had been devouring the inhabitants of the kingdom. The warrior Beowulf arrived on the scene and that very night lay in wait for Grendel in the king's great hall. The swamp monster arrived and was mortally wounded by the great warrior.

With the monster dead there was much celebration. But that night, as Beowulf and his men slept in a different part of the palace, an even greater monster came from the swamp and captured and killed the king's best friend. And who was this second swamp monster? It was the mother of Grendel.

With great courage and intuitive skill Beowulf followed this even more hideous monster into the deep water, and after a great battle, he killed her with a sword he found in her lair.

The moral of the story? Beware of not just the thing you fear—Grendel—but also that which gave birth to what you fear—the mother of Grendel. The creator of the monster is a more dangerous enemy than the monster itself.

Let me explain. I must admit I have always been an in-control kind of person. I work hard to keep life predictable. I seldom get lost on a trip because I always have several maps in my possession. I've studied them ahead of time and determined the best route. Sometimes I even commit the route to memory. I like to maintain the illusion that I am in control of my life. If the King of Denmark feared Grendel, the swamp monster, then the thing I fear is losing control of my life.

But the greater problem is not the thing I fear, but that which gave birth to the thing I fear. And what gives birth to my fear of losing control? What I fear most is the ultimate loss of control—death.

In his marvelous book, *The Denial of Death*, Earnest Becker said we live in a culture that does everything it can to deny the reality of death. But the fact is we all die. It is my own death I try to avoid by maintaining tight controls over my life. Beowulf found a way to face that which he feared most. How do I face the fear of death?

Thousands of years before Beowulf there were those who found the courage to face their deepest fears. One of them was David, a king who knew many a "swamp monster" in his day. He was also a king who found peace on the other side of fear. Listen to his words in Psalm 23 from *The New English Bible*:

The LORD is my shepherd;
　　I shall want nothing.
He makes me lie down in green pastures,
　　and leads me beside the waters of peace;
He renews life within me,
　　and for his name's sake guides me in the right path.
Even though I walk through a valley dark as death
　　I fear no evil, for thou art with me,
　　Thy staff and thy crook are my comfort.
Thou spreadest a table for me
　　in the sight of my enemies;
Thou has richly bathed my head with oil,
　　and my cup runs over.
Goodness and love unfailing,
　　these will follow me all the days of my life,
And I shall dwell in the house of the LORD
　　my whole life long.

We too can find courage and peace in the face of our monsters, because the Lord is with us.

—Paul S. Williams

What do you fear the most? Why?

What is the true source of your fears—the thing that gave birth to that which you fear? What promises does God give you in the Bible that will give you courage in the face of your "monsters"?

_____

_____

_____

_____

_____

_____

_____

_____

_____

_____

_____

_____

_____

peace

The Neighborhood Church

[Jesus said,] "For where two or three come together in my name, there am I with them."

THE NEIGHBORHOOD CHURCH

I was 4 when we moved out of the city of Syracuse, New York, and into the suburbs of Liverpool, New York, to Green Acres Drive. It was a great neighborhood to grow up in. The street seemed so much bigger then. Everything seemed bigger then.

A few years after we moved onto that street, a church was built on the corner. Our family didn't attend church very often. We went on Easter and never missed at Christmas. The minister at the new church was a kind and gracious man who stopped by our home a few times and invited us to attend, but we weren't interested.

I did, though, spend a lot of time there. The churchyard was the biggest lot around. We played football and baseball games there. The minister came out sometimes to watch, sometimes to play, and often just to break up arguments. He was surprisingly normal. He had kids, he laughed. He was even a pretty decent ball player. At the time I couldn't have told you any of that about him. But looking back, this man of faith, who let some kids use the church as a place to play, made a real impression on me.

The minister of that small church was a simple man of faith with a great heart who truly cared about people. He took time to play with us neighborhood kids in the churchyard, even if we didn't attend services there. He rolled up his sleeves and joined us, with a hearty laugh and a fast arm to first base. He often invited us to attend youth events at the church. Sometimes I went. One summer a neighbor invited me to go to a week of camp the church sponsored. My parents said yes, and I headed into New York's Finger Lakes region to a place that changed my life.

I gave my life to Christ at that week of camp. And when I came home I joined with the Christians to worship in that little church on my street. It wasn't long before my sister and parents started attending with me. We joined other families there on the journey of faith, all trying to follow Jesus the best we could. It was a community of grace.

When I was growing up, that church seemed very big to me, maybe because so much of my spiritual formation began there or because so many of the most important decisions of my life were made there. Or maybe it was because the people who started me on the spiritual journey were, in fact, giants of the faith.

There are thousands of churches like the one in Liverpool, New York, dotting the landscape of the world. They are communities of faith that make a difference in the lives of the people who play ball in the churchyard, come to know the kindhearted people inside, and commit themselves to traveling together on the spiritual journey. The next time you drive by the neighborhood church, maybe you ought to stop and go inside. It might just change your life.

—Rick Rusaw

Do you attend church? Why or why not? If you do, what brought you to your church?

What things might you do to help others feel welcomed into your church family?

_____

_____

_____

_____

_____

_____

_____

_____

_____

_____

_____

_____

_____

The Sand, the Stars, and Me

How precious to me are your thoughts, O God!

How vast is the sum of them!

Were I to count them,

they would outnumber the grains of sand.

PSALM 139:17, 18

THE SAND, THE STARS, AND ME

I would like to count all the grains of sand in the entire world. Really, I would. A friend of mine, Zach, has already started the count by numbering 1,850 grains of sand per one-eighth of a teaspoon. That equals 710,400 grains per cup. So, I'm set. I just need to count the miles of seashore for the seven continents, which is doable, and convert those miles into cups and multiply by 710,400.

But wait, I suppose that is just surface sand. I would need to estimate how deep the beaches are, and how far out into the oceans I need to go. And I can't forget the deserts, thousands of square miles of deserts. How deep and wide do they measure? I'm not so sure my goal is achievable after all. But it's a valuable project. Really, it is!

If you've ever felt alone, felt that no one cared about you, you could count the grains of sand and know how deep and wide God loves you. Psalm 139 says that the thoughts of God number more than the grains of sand in the whole earth! Even one cup of God's thoughts toward us is more than 700,000 thoughts, which is one thought every minute for a year and four months!

In Estes Park, Colorado, you can visit Rocky Mountain National Park where there are hundreds of thousands of square acres of mountains, forests, and rivers. It is a breathtaking and spectacular place. But the Rocky Mountains are just a tiny speck on the map of Colorado, and Colorado is just one of the 50 United States. The United States is only one-third of the North American continent, and our continent is just one of seven. And the seven continents make up only one-third of the earth's mass, two-thirds being water. And the earth is a tiny planet in our universe.

The sun is much bigger, at the center of a vast galaxy we call the Milky Way, just one among many galaxies, spinning around its center at 155 miles per second.

I love statistics and find them to be really important sometimes. I like to use them to consider how huge the universe is—too big to get our telescopes and imaginations around. And yet, God simply spoke it all into being. Statistics haven't been created that can even begin to describe our magnificent God.

Remember: there are 700,000 grains of sand per cup and it would take 200 million years to fly around the Milky Way one time. And yet, in all this vastness, God noticed us personally. Oh, to be noticed by the one who cannot be truly fathomed, to have the creator of the Milky Way think of you more times than there are grains of sand. It's not the statistics that overwhelm me; it is the truth to which they point. God is wild about us— and that is a wild thought!

—*Greg Allen*

What are your thoughts as you consider the vastness of our universe and the unfathomable numbers it would take to quantify it?

What are your feelings when you realize that the creator of the entire universe loves you personally?

_____

_____

_____

_____

_____

_____

_____

_____

_____

_____

_____

_____

A Man Convicted Against His Will

[Jesus said.] "The thief comes only to steal and kill and destroy; I have come that [my followers] may have life, and have it to the full."

JOHN 10:10

A MAN CONVICTED AGAINST HIS WILL

"A man convicted against his will is of the same opinion still."
I'm not sure when I heard that quotation for the first time, but it
stuck with me. People don't like being told what they cannot do.
That is a fundamental principle of human nature. Yet, there will
always be folks who think their job is to tell us what we can or
can't do. Most of the time it doesn't even matter if they're right
or wrong. We both know that when they tell us "you can't do that,"
we'll do our best to find a way to do it. A very strong-willed
woman in our nation's history devoted much of her life, rather
unsuccessfully, to telling Americans what they could not do.

Carrie Amelia Moore Nation stood 6 feet tall. She packed a
strong will to match her brawn. She was born in Kentucky in
1846. Carrie moved to Kansas and there discovered that her
new state was not enforcing a law prohibiting the sale of intoxi-
cating beverages, or "demon rum," as it would come to be
called. This did not make Carrie Nation very happy because her
first husband had died an alcoholic. So she took up her own
personal crusade of ridding, not just Kansas, but the entire
country, of alcohol.

You'll find this a bit difficult to believe, but it's true. Carrie Nation,
all 6 feet of her, took an axe and, with the law technically on her
side, personally smashed every tavern in Wichita, Kansas. I'm
telling you the truth. Then it was on to Topeka, then St. Louis
and Chicago, all the way out to California and back to New York.
Lawmakers were toppled who didn't hold tightly to the law, as
she demanded. Her temperance and woman's suffrage move-
ment swept the country. Incredibly, she managed to orchestrate
an amendment to the United States Constitution that made it
illegal to sell alcoholic beverages anywhere in America.

Remember, though: "A man convicted against his will is of the same opinion still." There would soon be another constitutional amendment that rescinded the first. Carrie Nation's second husband filed for divorce, saying she had abandoned him on her crusade. This woman who devoted much of her life telling people "you can't" died alone and penniless as the main character in an odd drama.

Carrie Nation and I probably would not have gotten along very well. You see, I'd much rather be known by what I am *for*, than by what I'm *against*. I suppose that's why the Bible is my favorite book in the whole world. Surprised? Most people think of it as some kind of rule book, God's list of don'ts. But the exact opposite is true. The theme of God's Word is freedom. He says, "Live the way I'm suggesting and you will know blessing and balance and health and peace." The God of the Bible is not some cosmic spoilsport, but one who loves life and freedom, and loves us too. The Christian life isn't about what God's against. It's about what he's for. And what he's for is a fulfilling life for me and for you.

—Dan Stuecher

Have you ever been told not to do something and found yourself wanting to do that very thing because you were told no? Why do you think that is?

_____

_____

_____

_____

_____

_____

_____

_____

_____

_____

_____

_____

_____

How does it change your perspective on living the Christian life when you realize that God is more interested in you living a full life than in making sure you follow a lot of rules?

_____

_____

_____

_____

_____

_____

135

_____

_____

_____

_____

_____

_____

_____

The Voice of God

You show that you are a letter from Christ . . . written not with ink but with the Spirit of the living God, not on tablets of stone but on tablets of human hearts. Such confidence as this is ours through Christ before God.

2 CORINTHIANS 3:3, 4

THE VOICE OF GOD

We can only read their words, but we will never hear them speak. We are left to experience the strength, wisdom, reassurance, or even dread of their thoughts preserved on the printed page, but we will never hear the pitch, timbre, or rhythm of their voices. They lived before the technology that would allow us to capture the sound of their speech. Haven't you wondered what it would have been like to hear Lincoln speak at Gettysburg, Washington offer his farewell address, Napoleon challenge his troops before battle, Jenny Lind enthrall an audience with her singing voice, or even Jesus as he taught on the hillside?

As fascinating as it would be to be able to hear them, we really don't need their voices. What they've left us is more than enough. An incident near the end of the life of the classical composer Johannes Brahms underscores that thought.

In 1890 Brahms was a dinner guest at the home of friends, along with Theodore Wangemann who was Thomas Edison's European agent. Wangemann was demonstrating Edison's new invention (called the cylinder recording machine) by collecting the voices of famous men and women. Brahms had always been fascinated by new inventions, and he turned excitedly to face the large, cone-shaped trumpet of the new recording device. His voice squeaks in German as he compliments Edison, and then there follows a minute of the composer playing the piano. It is the only recording of Brahms that exists. It is the stuff of legend, in some small way linking us with the great classical composers of long ago.

But the tinny sound of that primitive recording of Brahms's voice is not his legacy. We discover Brahms not through his voice, but through his music, which was the very essence of his life. He couldn't possibly have known that the invention before him, which then was little more than a toy, would eventually make it possible for him to "speak" to us through his music and allow us to come to know him very well.

God's voice has never been recorded. The most sophisticated recording equipment known to man has never captured the sound of God's vocal cords. He doesn't need to speak audibly though. He knows how to communicate far more effectively. The Bible says that God writes his words on our hearts. We come to know God not through hearing a voice but through knowing his Word.

That Bible you may not open very often is much more than just another book you're supposed to read. It is alive. It is literally God communicating himself to you. This is what he has chosen to give of himself to us; this is how he wants to stay in touch with us; and it is more than enough. Read it, believe it, and live it. That will be your message back to him.

—*Dan Stuecher*

Whose voice do you wish had been recorded so you could hear it now? Why?

Take a few moments to be still before God. What does he seem to be saying to you right now?

The Cross: Ugly or Beautiful?

For the message of the cross is foolishness to those who are

perishing, but to us who are being saved it is the power of God.

1 CORINTHIANS 1:18

THE CROSS: UGLY OR BEAUTIFUL?

If a resident of the ancient Roman Empire could walk our streets today, he would be utterly appalled to see crosses everywhere—on church buildings, in church sanctuaries, plastered on billboards and T-shirts, standing out in fields as stark monuments, and hanging around our necks as jewelry. His experience would be comparable to you or me coming back to life in a thousand years and hearing religious people sing about electric chairs or seeing miniature electric chairs crafted out of expensive silver or gold and worn as necklaces. So what, if anything, do you think about when *you* see the cross today?

Personally, I think we may be missing the point of the cross. Our contemporary culture has crafted, shaped, polished, and sanitized our symbols of the cross to the point where we have lost sight of what it was originally designed to accomplish. We simply do not grasp the unspeakable horror that occurred on crosses. Seventy years before Jesus walked the footpaths of Galilee, Roman legions smashed the revolt of Spartacus, and history tells us the roads to Rome were lined with 6,000 crosses, men dying on each of them. At the death of Herod the Great, insurrection broke out in the streets of Jerusalem, and Roman soldiers crucified over 2,000 people in the city. In A.D. 70 during the siege of Jerusalem, Roman troops crucified as many as 500 Jews daily for several months. Ask the families of any one of those thousands, and they would find it impossible to understand how we could come to revere such an ugly instrument of death. Crucifixion still stands among the cruelest, most inhumane methods of execution ever devised.

So I'll ask you again: what, if anything, do you think about when you see the cross today? Is a cross used for crucifixion ugly or beautiful? I think the answer depends on whom you ask and who is being crucified. Tens of thousands have been crucified, but only one cross is the pivotal point of history. When we understand the cross of Jesus in all its ugliness, as a symbol of God becoming man and dying for sin, it becomes stunningly beautiful. However, when we try to make it beautiful by ignoring its meaning, when we refuse to acknowledge what was accomplished on it, when we only light it up, shine it up, and talk it up, it becomes indescribably ugly again.

No matter what terrible mistakes may be in our pasts, when we understand that Jesus paid for them all through the tortuous agony of the cross, we then discover the beauty of freedom from guilt, the meaning to life, and peace with God.

So whether you wear it around your neck, paste it on your car, or stick it on top of a building, remembering the cross's ugly use points us to its beautiful meaning.

—Dan Stuecher

What is your opinion on the cross? Is it ugly or beautiful? Why?

_____

_____

_____

_____

_____

_____

_____

_____

_____

_____

_____

_____

_____

_____

How can you keep the message of the cross at the forefront, so that the symbol doesn't lose its meaning in your life?

_____

_____

_____

_____

_____

_____

147

_____

_____

_____

_____

_____

_____

_____

The Words Don't Matter

It is good to praise the LORD

and make music to your name, O Most High,

to proclaim your love in the morning

and your faithfulness at night,

to the music of the ten-stringed lyre

and the melody of the harp.

For you make me glad by your deeds, O LORD;

I sing for joy at the works of your hands.

PSALM 92:1-4

THE WORDS DON'T MATTER

I cut my teeth on southern gospel music. The tight harmonies sounded like Heaven to me. While other junior high kids were hanging Beatles posters in their lockers, I was listening to the Stamps Quartet. I worked as a radio announcer in high school. While other DJs were interviewing Blood, Sweat & Tears, I was interviewing Terry Blackwood of the Imperials. As far as I was concerned, it was all about the vocal harmonies.

Music has always been important to me. During my 20s I was with a couple of music groups that made albums. We focused on tight harmonies. But I have a confession to make: I almost never listen to the words of music. I never have. All I hear is the music itself. My wife always says "Wow, don't those words just grab you?"

"What are the words?" I answer.

The sound of the music itself is so rich to my ears it leaves no room for words. I can listen to the harmonies in a song over and over until I know every single part. But I don't have a clue what the words are. But you see, for me, that's OK. I don't need the words. I find God in the harmony.

Even in the days when I was not sure God existed, every now and then it seemed like he might be whispering to me through musical harmony. And it doesn't have to be religious music. Bluegrass, country, jazz, or even barbershop quartets will do.

Some people think it's crazy that my musical ear gets so caught up in the harmony that it can't hear the words. But if God is in the harmony, then I'm in good company.

Isn't that what the Trinity is all about—God as harmony—Father, Son, and Spirit? Harmonies are musical notes relating to one another in a way that's pleasing to the ear. The Father, Son, and Spirit relate to one another in a way that's pleasing our souls. When I hear musical harmony, it sounds godly by its very nature. As long as I have ears to hear voices raised in harmony, I'll know God is in his Heaven, and I'm in his hands.

—Paul S. Williams

Do you listen more to the lyrics of songs or more to the music? Why? What types of music cause your heart and soul to turn to God? Why?

Think about the comparison of musical harmony to the harmony of the Trinity. How do you think they are similar?

_____

_____

_____

_____

_____

_____

153

_____

_____

_____

_____

_____

_____

A Long Journey

How long, O LORD? Will you forget me forever?

  How long will you hide your face from me?

How long must I wrestle with my thoughts

  and every day have sorrow in my heart?

How long will my enemy triumph over me?

  Look on me and answer, O LORD my God.

Give light to my eyes, or I will sleep in death;

  my enemy will say, "I have overcome him,"

  and my foes will rejoice when I fall.

But I trust in your unfailing love;

  my heart rejoices in your salvation.

I will sing to the LORD,

  for he has been good to me.

PSALM 13

A LONG JOURNEY

It is said that in the ancient world all roads led to Rome. Many who made the journey came in freedom. Some came for commerce. Others were looking for a place to call home. But for many others who came to the shores of the Mediterranean, Rome was not a pleasant sight at all. It was the end of an awful journey, the place where, as prisoners, those weary travelers would come before Caesar and their fate for this earthly life would be made known. Many remained prisoners in small rooms for a very long time. One of them was the apostle Paul.

On his way to Rome Paul had been transferred from one ship to another. One ship was in a place called Fair Havens, getting ready to set sail for the harbor at Phoenix, in Crete. Paul appealed to the captain and owner of the ship and begged them not to sail. He said there were terrible storms on the Adriatic Sea this time of year. But Paul was a prisoner. Why should they listen to him?

They set sail. Three days out, a "northeaster" kicked up with hurricane force winds. They could make no headway against the storm, so they hoisted the lifeboat and lashed it tightly to the deck. They passed ropes under the ship itself to hold it together. They lowered the sea anchor, but with the storm still raging the next day, every appearance was that the ship would be destroyed. They started throwing cargo overboard. The next day they threw the ship's tackle into the sea. Finally, they lost all hope of being saved (Acts 27:8-20).

The ship ran aground on a sand bar and began to break apart. Everyone who couldn't swim rode pieces of the destroyed ship to shore. They drifted onto the island of Malta. They stayed three months until an Alexandrian ship brought them to Puteoli. From there Paul continued to Rome, but his storm was just beginning (Acts 27:41–28:16).

Finally in Rome, Paul was allowed to live by himself with a soldier to guard him. For two years he remained in a rented house in Rome, where the book of Acts says he "preached the kingdom of God and taught about the Lord Jesus Christ" (Acts 28:17-31).

But during that time Paul's friends deserted him. He was left imprisoned, far from their minds. At Paul's first defense against those who had imprisoned him, not one single person came to his support.

Not exactly a charmed life. Betrayed by his fellow countrymen, arrested, and turned over to the Roman authorities, he almost died during a shipwreck. He was threatened with death by the sailors, risked his life on Malta, then risked his life again in Rome. Yet after all this, no one came to his defense. Worse yet, those who had been his friends all deserted him. I can only imagine how utterly alone Paul must have felt as he lay in his bed, a prisoner of Rome.

But, in spite of it all, Paul knew that his God had not abandoned him. He wrote, "The Lord stood at my side and gave me strength, so that through me the message might be fully proclaimed" (2 Timothy 4:17).

Paul died as a martyr for his faith in Christ. But he, like David, had already come to realize that as terrible as the suffering on this earth might be, death was not the final word. The Lord was the final word.

Paul had found a reason to live and something worth dying for. Many people live sad and desperate lives, never once encountering something for which they'd give their lives. Paul knew that, regardless of the end he might meet not far from his Roman cell, God would rescue him from every evil and bring him safely to his heavenly kingdom. And for Paul, that was enough.

—*Paul S. Williams*

We won't all experience the perils that Paul did, but we all do experience suffering. What difficult trials have you experienced lately?

_____

_____

_____

_____

_____

_____

_____

_____

_____

_____

_____

_____

_____

How does Paul's story of faith through shipwrecks, imprisonment, and abandonment bring you hope in the face of your suffering?

_____

_____

_____

_____

_____

_____

_____

_____

_____

_____

_____

_____

_____

Pressed

Jesus went out as usual to the Mount of Olives, and his disciples
followed him. On reaching the place, he said to them, "Pray that
you will not fall into temptation." He withdrew about a stone's
throw beyond them, knelt down and prayed, "Father, if you are
willing, take this cup from me; yet not my will, but yours be
done." An angel from heaven appeared to him and strengthened
him. And being in anguish, he prayed more earnestly, and his
sweat was like drops of blood falling to the ground.

LUKE 22:39-44

PRESSED

The word *garden* can prompt different mental images in different people. If you grew up on a farm, the garden may bring back memories of hours spent pulling weeds or building scarecrows. Hopefully, those same memories will make your mouth water as you recall the tastes of sweet corn, huge ripe tomatoes, and green beans.

If your family roots are European, the idea of a garden may mean something else altogether. The aristocracy and royal families of Europe designed huge gardens to showcase their wealth and create remarkable environments for privacy, reflection, and beauty.

Interestingly, if you could have had the opportunity to say the word *garden* to Jesus, it would probably have meant both ideas to him. His garden was a beautiful place where olives were grown and processed for oil, as well as a place that provided a retreat for privacy and prayer. Say *garden* to Jesus and it could only mean one place: Gethsemane.

You would have had to cross a short bridge over a small valley east of Jerusalem to reach the garden. The brook beneath that bridge was called *Kidron*, a word that meant "dark or murky." The water had a distinctly red tint during the season of Passover because it flowed underneath the temple, and during the Passover week the blood from the sacrifices would seep down and blend with the waters. I wonder if, as Jesus looked down into that water the day before his death, he thought about his own blood mingling with the water of the Brook Kidron.

The word *Gethsemane* literally means "olive press"—where the very life of the fruit is squeezed out. And this would be the place where the agony of anticipating the cross would literally press the lifeblood from Jesus' body in a sweat of anxiety few have known. Here he would be faced with a choice: submission or resistance. Would he comply with the plan God had already set in motion or would he resist and challenge his Father's will? That's the same pressure-packed choice confronting us, isn't it? In the "press" of Gethsemane Jesus faced the challenge of the cross. In the press of our daily lives we face the challenge of choosing Christ over ourselves.

The Son asked the Father to spare him from the horror of the cross, but immediately followed this request with the words, "Not my will, but yours be done." It is a timeless, unfailing precedent worth following. You always will discover that the reward for submission to the Father far outweighs whatever sacrifice you are called to make, no matter how extreme you think it is. Just ask Jesus.

—Dan Stuecher

What challenge are you facing? What struggle, decision, or problem has you feeling "pressed"?

Will you submit yourself to God's plan though it may cost you dearly, or will you resist his will?

Doubting

Keep yourselves in God's love as you wait for the mercy of our Lord Jesus Christ to bring you to eternal life. Be merciful to those who doubt.

JUDE 21, 22

DOUBTING

I grew up in the church. My father was a minister. My uncle was a minister. Another uncle was the president of a Christian college. My brother became a minister. My cousins married ministers. There should be little surprise that I was ordained into Christian ministry.

But in spite of all that time in Sunday school, youth group, worship services, and seminary, I still have doubts about God. I'm not talking about a passing moment or two. I mean serious unanswered questions. But at least I'm not alone. On many occasions David and other writers of the psalms wondered where God was and why he seemed so silent in the midst of their trials. They had doubts about God. And if you're breathing, you probably have doubts too.

Franz Kafka said "A book must be the axe for the frozen sea within us." I've enjoyed several "axe" books that have broken open the frozen seas of my own life. One such book is Frederick Buechner's *Wishful Thinking—A Theological ABC.* Listen to what Buechner says about doubts:

"Whether your faith is that there is a God or that there is not a God, if you don't have any doubts you are either kidding yourself or asleep. Doubts are the ants in the pants of faith. They keep it awake and moving."

Buechner's point is well taken. I'm equally as uncomfortable with the Christian who says he has no doubts as I am with the unbeliever who is quite sure there is no God at all. Last I checked we humans were simply not given the tools to arrive at such certainty—one way or the other.

No, whether we're living the life of faith or the life of unbelief, none of us can be absolutely sure about God. I'm glad I've allowed my doubts to come to the surface. As such, they have become what Buechner calls "the ants in the pants of faith." They keep it moving. And because I've chosen to face those doubts, they have taken me to a deeper place than I might have known if I had never faced them. They have led me to a richer faith, to a place where I can embrace the mystery of God.

James 1:5, 6 is often misunderstood. At first glance it seems to indicate that we should never have any doubts about God: "If any of you lacks wisdom, he should ask God, who gives generously to all without finding fault, and it will be given to him. But when he asks, he must believe and not doubt, because he who doubts is like a wave of the sea, blown and tossed by the wind." But that is not what the passage says. What it suggests is that we *do something* about the doubts we have; that we wrestle with the questions of faith and belief in God, instead of leaving our doubts on the fringes of our lives.

169

May we face our doubts about God head-on, so that we may know the truth. Go ahead—wrestle with God. Ask him the big questions. He can handle it. If you do, you'll find yourself in a deeper place— a place where wisdom abides.

—*Paul S. Williams*

What are your doubts about God? Write them down here.

Take some time to look through your Bible and search for answers to your doubts. Write down anything that you learn. Pray that God will guide you and give you the answers you need.

_____

_____

_____

_____

_____

_____

_____

_____

_____

_____

_____

_____

_____

Confession

Then I acknowledged my sin to you

and did not cover up my iniquity.

I said, "I will confess

my transgressions to the LORD"—

and you forgave

the guilt of my sin.

PSALM 32:5

CONFESSION

You'd love little Johnny. He's 9 years old, energetic, creative, and all smiles. His third grade teacher says he's delightful. His classmates want to sit by him, his parents adore him, and even his older sister likes him. But Johnny's not perfect.

His teacher asked Johnny to go to the school office and bring back a notebook she had left there—the notebook that contained the math test she was about to give her class.

On his way back to the classroom Johnny couldn't stand it and peeked inside the notebook—and saw not only the test, but also the answer sheet. He walked a little slower now, slow enough to memorize the answers. Johnny got a perfect score, but he felt so guilty he was miserable. Within a week, he told his teacher what he'd done. And with that, Johnny had learned one of life's most important lessons.

Then there is Kyle—the nicest guy you'd ever want to meet. He was a successful businessman and a great family man, but Kyle was also guilt-ridden. He had stolen money from his company to support his gambling habit. It took the company a few months to find out, but then Kyle was prosecuted and sent to prison. But in prison he said this: "I'm so glad I don't have to lie anymore. Even though I'm in prison, I've never felt more free. I only wish I had confessed my wrong instead of waiting to get caught."

Kyle knew that freedom comes with confession. And with his wrongdoing confessed, Kyle could start a new life. And he has. His family forgave him and even his company forgave him. And today Kyle is doing quite well. Suffice it to say, when he does something wrong nowadays, he doesn't hide it. He tells the truth.

I often wonder if there are many people like little 9-year-old Johnny and 58-year-old Kyle who know they have done wrong, and suffer the gnawing pains of guilt. Good people do bad things, you know. The question is, what do you do with your guilt?

First, remember guilt is *good*. You're accepting responsibility for your wrongdoing when you feel guilty. But the next step is equally important. You have to confess. Forgiveness won't come until you've confessed. And the main reason you must confess is for the health of your own soul. It can be good for the people you've offended to hear you ask for their forgiveness. But the main beneficiary of confession is you.

Johnny didn't care what grade he got after he told his teacher what he'd done. He was just glad to have the truth known. Kyle didn't care what job he took when he got out of prison. He was just glad everything was out in the open.

Johnny and Kyle both know the truth—confession, my friends, is good for the soul.

—*Greg Allen*

Is there something you need to confess? Begin the process by writing it down on these pages. Reflect on God's forgiveness and write a prayer of confession, thanking him for washing away your sin.

Have you wronged someone else? Write the name(s) here, and write out the confession you need to make. When will you make this confession to this person?

_____

_____

_____

_____

_____

_____

177

_____

_____

_____

_____

_____

_____

_____

_____

Look Up!

"Consider how the lilies grow. They do not labor or spin. Yet I tell you, not even Solomon in all his splendor was dressed like one of these. If that is how God clothes the grass of the field, which is here today, and tomorrow is thrown into the fire, how much more will he clothe you, O you of little faith! And do not set your heart on what you will eat or drink; do not worry about it. For the pagan world runs after all such things, and your Father knows that you need them. But seek his kingdom, and these things will be given to you as well.

"Do not be afraid, little flock, for your Father has been pleased to give you the kingdom. Sell your possessions and give to the poor. Provide purses for yourselves that will not wear out, a treasure in heaven that will not be exhausted, where no thief comes near and no moth destroys. For where your treasure is, there your heart will be also."

LUKE 12:27-34

LOOK UP!

I am fortunate to live where the views are spectacular. The mountain views from the Front Range of Colorado are magnificent. On one recent morning, as the sun was rising over a slight dusting of snow on Long's Peak, the play of light on the mountains was amazing. I happened to see that scene as I was walking my dog, Bailey, in the park near our home. Our dog is a 10-month-old pug. She delights in any opportunity to take a walk. As we walked that morning I couldn't help but notice the difference between my pug and me (some might suggest there really isn't much difference). She was head down, exploring all the sights and smells along the sidewalk—she never once noticed the lake, the sunrise, or the wondrous peaks in the distance. While I was taking in the beauty, she was taking care of business.

It is so easy to let the trivial become important and the important become ordinary. Jesus was asked once, "What must I do to see God?" His answer was similar to this: "What blocks your view? Look up! Look around! Do you see how your life is consumed with your pursuits? If you are going to make the journey you will have to rearrange what matters most to you" (see Matthew 19:16-22).

While taking Bailey for that walk, I realized that I'm not much different from my dog on most days. I have a path to follow, business to attend to, head down, focused on the stuff right in front of me, oblivious to what God has in store. As hard as I try, sometimes in the midst of my pursuit of God, I get too focused on the trail. That isn't to suggest there isn't a need for me to focus on the daily routines of life. The problem comes when that is all I focus on.

I need to learn not to be so head down and focused on the business at hand that I miss out on what matters most. If the truth were told, I often ignore the view of the mountains, even though with just a glance out my front door, they are always right there—majestic and breathtaking.

I probably would have missed the beautiful scene that morning not long ago, but my wife was out of town, and the dog needed to be walked. And on the journey, I just happened to look up and see the splendor. Boy, am I glad. I wonder how many other times in my life God's been trying to get my attention—"Rick, look up!" he says. But I keep my head down, hard at work, trying to impress God and everybody with my great accomplishments. But if I'd only look up, I'd see God's already done a work far beyond anything I can imagine.

—*Rick Rusaw*

What things in your life have you looking down and preoccupied? Take a few minutes to look up and focus on Jesus. Look outside or take a walk. What beautiful things have you been missing by keeping your "nose to the ground"?

Devotions in this book are based on scripts first delivered by Paul S. Williams and the following hosts for *Worship.*

GREG ALLEN is a worship minister at Southeast Christian Church in Louisville, Kentucky, where he has served since 1983.

RICK RUSAW is senior minister at LifeBridge Christian Church in Longmont, Colorado, where he has served since 1991.

DAN STUECHER is senior minister at Harborside Christian Church in Safety Harbor, Florida, a congregation he founded in 1984.

■■
WINDOWS OF WORSHIP™

ISBN 0-7847-1514-9 • 25001

ISBN 0-7847-1515-7 • 25002

ISBN 0-7847-1516-5 • 25003

ISBN 0-7847-1517-3 • 25004

ISBN 0-7847-1518-1 • 25005

Perfect for personal reflection.
Ideal to give to a friend.
You will find many times when
Windows of Worship™ devotional
journals are just the right choice.